# ROUNDIN

D1561897

Dramatic Publishing
Woodstock, Illinois • England • Australia • New Zealand

For Rebecca and Sam

## IMPORTANT BILLING AND CREDIT REQUIREMENTS

All producers of the play *must* give credit to the author(s) of the play in all programs distributed in connection with performances of the play and in all instances in which the title of the play appears for purposes of advertising, publicizing or otherwise exploiting the play and/or a production. The name of the author(s) *must* also appear on a separate line, on which no other name appears, immediately following the title, and *must* appear in size of type not less than fifty percent the size of the title type. Biographical information on the author(s), if included in the playbook, may be used in all programs. *In all programs this notice must appear:*

Produced by special arrangement with
THE DRAMATIC PUBLISHING COMPANY of Woodstock, Illinois

One day my son, Sam, came home from Little League practice and announced that his coaches had provided the team with new strategy for the upcoming playoffs. When one of the slower kids on the team got on base, he'd receive a signal which meant that upon reaching the next base, he should slide and pretend to be injured. That way, the coaches could take him out of the game and replace him

with a faster runner. When Sam said, "Coach, isn't that cheating?" the coach replied, "No, Sam, that's called strategy."

I was horrified. Is this how our children are being trained to deal with competition? How many future Enrons are brewing on our Little League fields and in our school gyms under the watchful eyes of over-zealous coaches? What about building character and encouraging fair play? Or are such notions laughable in this country at this point in history? At that moment I knew that I had to write *Rounding Third*. But, as the play was germinating in my head, I found myself thrust more intimately into the fray, first as an assistant coach and then as the coach of my son's team.

Philosophically, there was no question about where I stood. Little League should be fun and the kids should be encouraged to progress at their own speed, free of the overwhelming pressure that awaits them in practically every aspect of their lives, just around the corner.

And yet, when I found myself actually coaching, I discovered that I wanted to win. I really wanted to win. That voice I heard bellowing across the diamond was, sadly, my own. Perhaps to rationalize the extent of these feelings, I concluded that since we

5

live in such a highly competitive society, don't we have an obligation to teach our children how to succeed? Given that this is the arena where they will be playing out their lives, shouldn't we equip them with the tools it takes to win?

By the time I wrote the play, I believed passionately in these opposing points of view. We should protect and nurture our children during this brief, precious time in their lives. And we should teach them how to compete and how to win.

The two mismatched coaches in *Rounding Third*, the "win at all costs" Don and the "can't we just have fun?" Michael, reflect this conflict. In my mind, they never agree and they are both right. And as they struggle to communicate their opposing philosophies to the team, they reveal who they are. The play ultimately became an exploration of what it is to be a man in this culture, how having children changes one's self-perceptions, and what it truly means to succeed.

Now, when I hear Don's exhortations to the team—which are delivered directly to the audience—I hear the voices of the many coaches I've had, starting with my first year of Little League. And I hear my own voice, more impatiently than I'd like, instructing, imploring, urging the team on to victory.

And when I hear Michael encouraging the team after a tough loss or fervently praying for his own hapless son to catch his first fly ball of the season, I hear the hopefulness and the innocence that seems both entirely appropriate and somewhat out of touch.

The horror I felt at hearing my son's description of his coach's "strategy" provided a powerful trigger to write a play. But writing the play was an act of discovery, reflecting my own conflicts about how we live with some kind of dignity and raise our children in a culture so ruthlessly obsessed with material success.

— *RD*

*Photo of Rick and Sam Dresser by Mike Disciullo*

# ROUNDING THIRD

A Play in Two Acts
For 2 Men

## CHARACTERS

DON, a man

MICHAEL, a man

TIME: Next season

PLACE: A small town near a big city in the United States of America.

The play is performed on a set featuring a ballfield with a bench, a bar, a van and a school gym.

The Northlight Theatre in Chicago, Illinois, presented the premiere production of ROUNDING THIRD on October 15, 2002. The production was directed by BJ Jones and included the following artists:

Don ................................ GEORGE WENDT
Michael ........................... MATHEW ARKIN

## PRODUCTION STAFF

Set Design......................... TODD ROSENTHAL
Lighting Design...................... CHRIS BINDER
Sound Design....................... LINDSAY JONES
Production Stage Manager ............... LAURA D. GLENN

ROUNDING THIRD opened off-Broadway at the John Houseman Theater in New York City on October 7, 2003. It was produced by Eric Krebs, Ted Tulchin, Robert G. Bartner and Chase Mishkin in association with M. Kilburg Reedy. The production was directed by John Rando and featured the following artists:

Don ................................ ROBERT CLOHESSY
Michael ........................... MATHEW ARKIN

## PRODUCTION STAFF

Set Design......................... DEREK MCLANE
Lighting Design ..................... F. MITCHELL DANA
Original Music ....................... ROBERT REALE
Sound Design....................... JILL B.C. DUBOFF
Production Stage Manager ................ JACK GIANINO
General Management .......... EKTM/JONATHAN SHULMAN
Casting Consultant...................... BARRY MOSS
Press Representative ... JEFFREY RICHARDS ASSOCIATES/IRENE
GANDY
Production Supervision.......... PETER FEUCHTWANGER/PRF
PRODUCTIONS

# ACT I

*(A BAR. DON is at a small table nursing a beer. MICHAEL enters.)*

DON. Are you Mike?

MICHAEL. Michael. Yes. You must be Donald.

DON. Don. Never Donald. Don.

MICHAEL. Great. Don. Well, hello. *(Sits down at the table.)* I'm not late, am I?

DON. No, no way. But let's not make a habit of it, okay?

MICHAEL. I got hung up at work. What a crazy day! I was trying to leave and something came up and I never thought I'd finish. Then, well, long story short, I finished.

DON. Nice going. You want something to drink?

MICHAEL. No, I'm fine. But thanks so much for asking.

DON. You honestly didn't know who I was when you showed up?

MICHAEL. We've never met. Have we?

DON. No. But I figured you'd know *of* me even if you didn't know me.

MICHAEL. You're pretty well known?

DON. Let's just say...yes. People who go out of their houses tend to know who I am. You're not a shut-in, are you, Mike?

MICHAEL. Michael. Oh, no. I get out a lot. Every single day.

DON. Good for you.

MICHAEL. I'm just new.

DON. That explains it. How new?

MICHAEL. A few months.

DON. Beautiful. Like it so far?

MICHAEL. Overall. People have been—

DON *(cutting him off).* That's just the kind of place it is. And the people get more like that the longer you stay. Sure you don't want a beer?

MICHAEL. Sorry.

DON. Don't apologize, man.

MICHAEL. Right.

DON. I mean if it's a problem, hell, it's a disease, some of my best friends, out of the bar, into the program, back to the wife, who are we to judge? But honestly, Mikey, just between you and me, they sure as hell aren't as much fun.

MICHAEL. I just don't want a beer, Don.

DON. You said that.

MICHAEL. I mean I don't have a problem, if that's what you're thinking.

DON. I'm not thinking anything. It's just interesting how you keep bringing it up.

MICHAEL. I want to be clear.

DON. Got it. But if you do have a problem, it's not your fault. Because it's a disease. You wouldn't blame someone for having cancer, would you, Mike?

MICHAEL. Not me.

DON. So I think we should be understanding rather than judgmental. I think that's important.

MICHAEL. I'm pretty sure we're on the same page.

DON. Well, enough preliminary chit-chat, let's get started.

MICHAEL. Perfecto!

DON. Incidentally, Mike, you and I will be spending a lot of time together. So if I choose to unwind with a beer, there's no need for an intervention. I don't have that particular disease. Just so we understand each other.

MICHAEL. This is not an issue with me. You do whatever you want to do.

DON. Thanks. Nice to get permission from the new guy. Mike, if there's one key to my own personal success it would be this: I draft well.

MICHAEL. Nice going! *(Beat.)* What exactly does that mean?

DON. Getting new kids on the team. My son, Jimmy, he watches the other kids play at school and he clues me in. Who the best prospects are, so we can be smart in the draft and not stupid. We're in sweet shape. Eight kids are coming back from last year. Which means we only draft four.

MICHAEL. That's good. A solid core of able-bodied returnees.

DON. I guess you could put it like that. Jimmy also helped me compile a list of kids to avoid.

MICHAEL. All the kids get on teams, right?

DON. Of course! Like I said, this is all about the kids. But the ones you'd like to avoid are the ones who'd rather be in *Brigadoon*, you know what I'm saying?

MICHAEL. Just as long as everyone gets a chance.

DON. Mike, you can relax. Your kid got a very good scouting report from my kid.

MICHAEL. Really? Wow. Don, that means a lot. I'm embarrassed.

DON. Why are you embarrassed?

MICHAEL. Look at me. My eyes are misting up. This is very emotional. This is big. I'm sorry. Whew.

DON *(long look, then to clipboard)*. Hits to all fields, strong arm, needs work on ground balls.

MICHAEL. How much work?

DON. Hey, it's Little League. All the kids have trouble with ground balls.

MICHAEL. Oh, good. Misery loves company. They'll miss the ball and strike out and run to the wrong base—

DON. Whoa! Not that.

MICHAEL. Not what?

DON. No one on my team runs to the wrong base. I'll never yell at the kids for physical errors, but mental errors, they'll get an earful. They need to learn the mental side of the game or what are we doing, Mike?

MICHAEL. Excuse me?

DON. We're jerking off.

MICHAEL. Oh.

DON. In which case we don't need to make schedules and practice—

MICHAEL. Definitely don't need to practice!

DON. What's that, Mike?

MICHAEL. I'm just saying…we don't need to practice…

DON. I'm afraid I don't understand. We don't need to practice?

MICHAEL. Jerking off.

DON *(long look, then turns to clipboard)*. Here's the other list. Philip Bailey, Douglas French, Arthur Camilli, Frank Nassiter-Wise…don't you just love the hyphenated kids?

MICHAEL. What exactly is this list, Don?

DON. Bottom line, these are kids we do not want on our team.

MICHAEL. I think we might have a little problem with Frank Nassiter-Wise.

DON. Oh, I'm sure we'd have many problems with Frank Nassiter-Wise if he ended up on the team. Which, may I say, is highly unlikely?

MICHAEL. He's my son.

DON. Frank Nassiter-Wise is your son?

MICHAEL. Yes, he is. And I was told he'd be on this team.

DON. You're Johnson. Mike Johnson.

MICHAEL. Michael Johnson.

DON. I thought Dan Johnson was yours. The kid that can hit to all fields.

MICHAEL. I'm Johnson. My son is Nassiter-Wise.

DON. How come?

MICHAEL. How come? Because of my wife's first marriage.

DON. Boy oh boy. My mistake. Somebody get this goddamn egg off my face.

MICHAEL. Don't worry about it.

DON. I just stepped in it up to my ass. Jesus Christ. Great start, huh?

MICHAEL. Really, Don, it's okay.

DON. But I have to say, in my own defense, it's pretty confusing. How come you didn't get your own name up there on the marquee along with Nassiter and Wise?

MICHAEL. I guess at a certain point the child starts to sound like a law firm.

DON. Mikey, baby, what can I say? We all love our kids, I didn't know he was your kid, I'm a big enough man to say I'm sorry. Even though I feel totally blind-sided by this whole Nassiter-Wise bullshit.

MICHAEL. Don't beat yourself up, Don. What concerns me is this policy of blackballing kids who don't have much experience.

DON. Nobody's blackballing anybody. My first obligation is to the kids. Every one of which will play, as long as they get there on time. But if I can field a better team, why shouldn't I do that? Wouldn't you rather win than lose, given the choice?

MICHAEL. Well…

DON. That's just common sense. So I talk to my son and you know kids, they shoot off their crazy little motor-mouths and act like experts—

MICHAEL. What did he say about Frank?

DON. Huh?

MICHAEL. What did your son say about my son?

DON. Said he's good. Good little player. Potential up the butt.

MICHAEL. Could I please see the clipboard?

DON. I'm sorry, Mike. There's stuff on this clipboard no other man will ever see.

MICHAEL. What did he say?

DON. You understand you are asking me to break a sacred covenant with my son?

MICHAEL. I'd like to know what was said.

DON. Your boy, Frank, apparently has areas where he could improve.

MICHAEL. Like…?

DON. Like hitting, fielding, running, throwing, general understanding of the game. Okay? Fact, I don't judge; all the kids need improvement. And rest assured every kid on my team will learn and grow and sportsmanship and fun and how much goddamn baseball has your son actually played?

MICHAEL. He's played some soccer.

DON. Okay. Good. I wouldn't say the skills are directly transferable...but, hey, silver lining, this makes the draft easier. We're only looking for three kids.

MICHAEL. There you go.

DON. Mike, full disclosure, I demand a lot from my assistant coach in terms of time and involvement. If this isn't as serious a commitment as the one you'd make to your job or your marriage, I would respectfully suggest you bow out.

MICHAEL. Thanks, but I want to make a contribution.

DON. All I'm saying is: take a night to think about it.

MICHAEL. I've already thought about it. That's why I'm here. But I appreciate your concern.

DON. You know what I'm saying. Kick it around in your mental mind. Go back and forth. Throw things up in the air and see where they land. Promise me that?

MICHAEL. I'm sorry, Don.

DON. You're telling me you won't even rethink it for me?

MICHAEL. I could tell you I'm going to rethink it but I'd be lying because I've already made my decision. I don't want to start out by lying to you, Don.

DON. Sure, that can come later. Then I have no choice but to grit my teeth and welcome you as my assistant coach. *(They shake hands.)*

MICHAEL. Thanks! Can't wait to roll up the old sleeve-a-rooneys and get started!

DON. So. I gotta pick up Chinese, Jimmy's at the orthodontist, wife's at group. You know, sometimes people do things, people you love and honest to God, you could choke the life right out of them and plant them under the pool and sleep like a baby, you know what I mean?

MICHAEL. Right.

DON. You do understand what I mean?

MICHAEL. I think so. I mean…in theory.

DON. Interesting. I can handle the draft solo, first practice is Saturday.

MICHAEL. There's still snow on the ground.

DON. We'll be in the school gym. You can tell a lot about a boy by the way he handles ground balls rocketing up at him off the gym floor.

MICHAEL. It's really going to be a great season, Coach.

DON. God willing, and if we got the pitching. Thanks for helping. A good assistant coach is a treasure. I know from the last three years. Tony Barone. What a prize. Dedication, commitment, excellent teaching skills, deep knowledge of the game. And very punctual.

MICHAEL. Sounds like there's only one Tony Barone, but I'll do my best, Coach.

DON. Good to hear. And Mike, please be on time. *(MICHAEL leaves.)*

*(A SCHOOL GYM. DON blows his whistle. Then he addresses the team [the audience] at the first practice. Nearby, baseball equipment is scattered next to a duffel bag.)*

DON *(continuing)*. Unfortunately, we don't have much time this morning. The Pep Club has the gym at ten, so I'll keep this brief. First, congratulations! You're the luckiest kids in town. You're on my team. I can promise you'll work hard, learn a lot, and have fun. How do we have fun playing baseball? One word. Winning. Winning is fun. Losing stinks. I hope that isn't new information. I don't have a lot of rules. The main one is this: I am in charge, and what I say goes, without any backtalk or eye-rolling or wise-guy questions. When I blow my whistle? *(He blows the whistle.)* You *run* to me. If you dawdle, no problem, you just don't play the next game. Get to the ballpark half an hour before game time. "Is twenty-nine minutes good enough, Coach?" Sorry. "It's my parents' fault I'm late." Tough. Have your parents talk to me and I don't think we'll have any problems, assuming you remain on the squad. If you ask to play a particular position—"Coach, can I play short-stop?"—I guarantee you won't play shortstop for five games. That's it for rules. I keep them to a minimum and I take them seriously. *(Checks out the team.)* I'm glad to see most of you are wearing the equipment we suggested. *(Picking someone out.)* Philip? Philip Bailey? It is Phil, isn't it? Nice going, remembering to wear the cup. F.Y.I., it's traditionally worn *inside* the pants. But that's an interesting look, it could catch on. Whoa, you can make that change later, Phil! *(Beat.)* Now, we all drop fly balls, miss grounders, make bad throws, that's baseball. Those are called physical errors, and I will never yell at you over physical errors. What is it called when we forget how many outs there are or throw to the wrong base? Anyone? Those are mental errors, and yes, my friends, you *will* hear from me about mental errors.

*(MICHAEL enters with two take-out cups of coffee.)*

MICHAEL. Hi, Coach Don. Hello, team! Looking sharp!

DON. Well, look who's here! Our brand new assistant coach. We'd about given up on you, Mike.

MICHAEL. Sorry. I guess I'm just a few minutes late.

DON. Eleven, but who's counting? *(To MICHAEL's son.)* Just find a seat in the bleachers, Frank. Oops! You okay?

MICHAEL. He couldn't find his glasses. I got you a mocha latte, Don. Extra foam, didn't know how you like it. *(MICHAEL gives DON the coffee.)*

DON. Much appreciated, Mike! Since this isn't the ladies' sewing club I think I'll save it for later. *(DON tosses the coffee into the trash.)*

MICHAEL. Don't care for the mocha? Or was it the latte?

DON. Cards on the table, Mike, I like plain old American coffee. But thanks anyway. *(To the team.)* Hey, anybody from last year remember how many times former assistant coach Tony was late? That's right. Once. *(To MICHAEL.)* Tony's a policeman. One day, stopping a burglary, he got himself shot in the groin area. What a sickening, bloody mess. He was ten minutes late to practice that day. So as long as you have a good excuse, you won't hear a peep from me. What's your excuse, Assistant Coach Mike?

MICHAEL. It was really unbelievable traffic.

DON. Fair enough, can't be helped. Unless of course you allow enough time to get here. I'm just outlining bullet points of what the kids can expect. *(MICHAEL's cell phone rings.)*

MICHAEL. Uh-oh. I think I have to take this. *(MICHAEL turns away and talks quietly on the phone. DON turns to the team.)*

DON. Assistant Coach Mike is helping us out by demonstrating things we shouldn't ever do. Like be late or take calls. I know some of you kids have your own cell phones—God knows what your parents are thinking—a lot of people should never have .kids, they don't take it seriously, they never say no, and gee, why is everyone on dope and pregnant and living off my tax dollars? My one rule is if I ever see you chatting on the phone, well, some of you from last year remember our little demonstration which proved that a cell phone doesn't have much of a chance against a Louisville Slugger. *(MICHAEL finishes his call.)* Everything copacetic, Assistant Coach Mike?

MICHAEL. Yes, thanks. My apologies. Had to put out a fire.

DON. Was it a real fire?

MICHAEL. Never again, Don. *(To the team.)* I guess I should introduce myself and say a few words. My name is Michael Johnson—

DON. You can call him Mike—

MICHAEL. Actually, I prefer Michael, but...whatever. You know when I was your age, I played in a great number of curling matches—

DON. Was that "curling," Mike?

MICHAEL. Yes, I spent part of my childhood in Canada—

DON. Oh, I'm sorry to hear that.

MICHAEL. That's where curling is popular—not important, just hopefully interesting, fun information—but what *is* important, and the point I'd like to make, is—

DON. Is "curling" where you push this rock along the ice and get out little brooms and try to make it stop?

MICHAEL. For the purposes of right now, yes, Don, the specific rules of curling aren't important. What I would like to say, briefly—

DON. "Briefly" is an excellent choice, Mike. Because the Pep Club is in the lobby tapping its feet and I'd like to whack a few ground balls at my kids—

MICHAEL. It's about competition. These curling matches were the most important thing in my life when I was ten years old. But I honestly don't remember who won. I remember playing. So what I want to say to you, with the benefit of hindsight and, well, "wisdom" might be overstating it, is this: the fun is in the playing, not the winning and the losing. That's what I hope you will take away from this experience and what you will treasure when you get to be my age. And I guarantee you this, people, win or lose, you will have one heckuva lot of fun!

DON. Thanks, Assistant Coach Mike, although I covered "fun" earlier, before you got here. Probably you were still stuck in that unbelievable traffic.

MICHAEL *(to the team)*. One other thing, this whole enterprise is about *you*. So please, let us know, for example, what position you'd most enjoy playing—

DON. Assistant Coach Mike! Great intro, interesting ideas, which I'd put in the "devil's advocate" category, and darn it, the Pep Club's at the door!

MICHAEL. That's about it from my end, gang. Let's play ball!

DON *(to the back of the house)*. Hey, Pepsters! Can we have ten minutes? I know pep is important, but these children are the future, and yes, I know you have a permit! *(To MICHAEL.)* Mike, could you make yourself useful and pack up our equipment, which, sadly, we did- n't get to use? *(To the team.)* Okay, guys, that's it. Ev- erybody goes home except you and you. Not you, *you*! *(MICHAEL starts packing the equipment—bats, balls, catcher's equipment, batting helmets—into a duffel bag. He can't get it all in.)*

MICHAEL. Are you sure everything fits into this bag, Don?

DON. Well, let's see, it did last year and the year before and the year before that…but maybe this year is differ- ent. *(Watches MICHAEL struggling with the equipment.)* Mike, would you be available for a coaches' meeting?

MICHAEL. Sure. When?

DON. Right now.

MICHAEL. Okay.

DON. Mike, you're not a baseball man, are you?

MICHAEL. To tell you the truth, I'm a bit of a late- comer—

DON. You got that right—

MICHAEL. But I've started to really enjoy the game.

DON. That's excellent. I have just one rule. You need to clear things through me before you go shouting them out willy-nilly to my team.

MICHAEL. What do you mean?

DON. I mean you can't be standing there as my assistant coach saying that winning doesn't matter. You just can't do that. Because that is bullshit.

MICHAEL. But that's how I feel. Look at the big picture, Don. Do you honestly remember who won and lost the games you played as a kid?

DON. When I was twelve I hit .456 with eighteen RBIs. We went 11 and 4 and we lost the championship game

10 to 9 when Billy Nathan got picked off third base with two outs in the bottom of the last inning. I still think about that, Mike. I think about it a lot. I was coming up to bat and if Billy hadn't wandered off the base in some kind of a goddamned dream state, I know for a fact I could have brought him home and we'd have gone on to win. I have replayed that scenario many times inside my head, I have orchestrated many possible outcomes, all of them overwhelmingly positive. But I never got the chance because Billy took the bat out of my hands. And when Billy Nathan ran for school board last year, I could not find it in my heart to vote for him, even though I have every reason to believe he is a good and honest man who happened to make a thoughtless mistake when he was eleven years old. So yes, I do remember.

MICHAEL. You have a very good memory.

DON. A lot of men remember these things, Mike. 'Course it might be different in the world of curling.

MICHAEL. I just want to make sure everyone has a good experience this year. Even the kids who wander off third base in a dream state. *(DON watches MICHAEL struggle to get the equipment in the bag.)*

DON. Can I give you just a little advice?

MICHAEL. Sure. I'm always looking for pointers.

DON. Try putting that catcher's mask in first. Then maybe everything will fit. Mike, your job isn't going to keep getting in the way, is it?

MICHAEL. No. This was a rough week. A lot of things coming at me, all at once.

DON. What exactly do you do?

MICHAEL. My company has a lot of government contracts. And those government fellows keep you dancing pretty good sometimes. But I would have to say I'm out of the woods, at least for a while.

DON. Well, I'm just a simple Joe who paints people's houses, so I can't say I understand what the hell you're talking about. But if you can steal a few minutes from "your company" we should find a little face-time to get you up to speed.

MICHAEL. You just say the word. *(He gets everything in the bag.)* Hey, thanks, Don. It all fits. Wow. I really appreciate it.

DON. Okay, let's not get all emotional here, we're not women.

MICHAEL *(struggles with the bag as DON starts off)*. Oh, Don? Should I put this in your car?

DON. Nah, you can hold onto it. That was the arrangement with Tony and it worked like a charm. Good meeting, Mike. *(MICHAEL starts off with the duffel bag. DON stays.)*

MICHAEL. Don? Aren't you coming? I thought we could walk to our cars together.

DON. I'm gonna work with Jimmy and Eric.

MICHAEL. Where?

DON. Over here on the sidelines. They can spare a little pep-free zone so a couple of kids can pitch.

MICHAEL. Should I stay and help?

DON. Oh, no, Mike, practice is over. Your work is done. *(To Jimmy and Eric.)* Full windup, don't overthrow! Jimmy, save the arm!

MICHAEL. Is this special attention or punishment?

DON. What does it look like to you, Mike? *(Yells to kids.)* Jimmy, stop screwing around or you're dead meat!

MICHAEL. It's hard to say.

DON. Coaching your own kid is one of the hardest things a man can do. Too tough, people will talk, too nice, it's playing favorites. Plus, the kid thinks every nugget of advice is a vicious personal attack.

MICHAEL. Why is Eric here?

DON. He's been goofing off so I made him stay.

MICHAEL. Sounds like punishment.

DON. That's baseball.

MICHAEL. I should tell you, as assistant coach, I think these kids need to have fun. All this pressure and discipline is going to squelch their natural enthusiasm. We don't want that, do we?

DON. We certainly don't, Mike. *(Yells.)* No curve balls, Eric! Or you'll find yourself in the spring musical!

MICHAEL. Let's let them play on their own. Explore their imaginations, be the proud captains of their own little ships—

DON. Mike, did you happen to notice Eric's eye-twitch?

MICHAEL. No, I didn't.

DON. His parents just had a nasty split and neither one will leave the house. Advice from their lawyers. Every day's trench warfare with Eric in the middle, looking for cover.

MICHAEL. Oh, boy. That's rough.

DON. His dad comes to all the games and yells about how disappointed he is. Gives everyone a nice boost. So when the eye-twitch is really bad, I make Eric stay after practice and we go out for pizza and he spends the night at our house. *(Yells.)* Eric! Put your damn shoes back on or you're outta here! I'm not playing!

MICHAEL. That's a nice thing you're doing, Don.

DON. No, it's my job. I'd like to drag his idiot parents out of the house and kick their asses. I mean, in every marriage you're hanging by a thread and half the time you regret the day you were born but that's no reason to quit. I'll see you, Mike.

MICHAEL. I'll be on time, I promise! *(MICHAEL drags the duffel bag off. His cell phone rings. On phone:)* Roger? Hi... *(Beat.)* Is there some reason you need it Monday? Of course I can do it, but it will take up the rest of my weekend, and I was planning to play ball— *(Beat.)* No, I understand completely. You'll see my report on your desk, first thing in the morning...

*(THE BALLFIELD. DON blows the whistle and addresses the team.)*

DON. You got butterflies? I know I do. Opening day is always like that. It's good to be nervous, it just means you want to do well. The only no-hitter I ever pitched, I was twelve years old, opening day, you know what I did before the game? Anyone from last year remember? That's right. Vomited like crazy. Then I wiped off my mouth and went to the mound and pitched the greatest game of my life. Okay, our equipment's prob'ly caught in traffic, so let's start with some stretching. *(DON starts some stretching exercises.)* Rusty, bend all the way over, how are you going to stop a ground ball like that? *(Beat.)* Then don't eat pancakes before the game. Philip, push your hat back, I can't even see your eyes! And tie those shoelaces!

*(MICHAEL enters with the duffel bag.)*

MICHAEL. Hey, guys! The big day is finally here!

DON. Here's the man with the bag! Right on the button, if we were starting late!

MICHAEL. I'm ten minutes early! You said the game's at noon!

DON. I guess you missed my one rule. Thirty minutes before game time, Mike. No sweat, my fault, should have re-mentioned it. Put down the bag and join us. You know how to do the Macarena?

MICHAEL. No, sorry.

DON. Do you live on this planet? Everyone knows the Macarena. It's easy!

MICHAEL. Are you, what, asking me to dance?

DON. Last year, Tony and I, whenever the kids were a little tight, we'd dance the Macarena. It loosened them up, became a ritual. It was a big reason we won the championship. *(DON demonstrates the Macarena.)* Go on, give it a shot, Mikey.

MICHAEL. I'm going to pass on the Macarena.

DON. Do it for the kids! Mike, don't be such a slug. Would it kill you to shake your booty?

MICHAEL. I just don't understand the point of shaking my booty at this juncture… *(MICHAEL's cell phone rings.)*

DON. Do you really have to take it, Mike?

MICHAEL. I'm afraid I do. Rough week at work.

DON *(to team)*. Assistant Coach Mike has an important job running his own company. But I like to think what we're doing here is important, too! Grab a ball and start loosening up! Mike, would you give 'em some fungoes? *(MICHAEL's attention is torn between DON and the phone call.)*

MICHAEL. Fungoes?

DON. Damn! I thought old Tony might drop by. He's the master of fungoes.

MICHAEL. If you show me where the fungoes are I'll be happy to give them out.

DON. Fungoes are fly balls, Mike. Do you think you can hit a few?

MICHAEL. No problem. *(Finishes call and grabs a bat.)* I'm on it!

DON. You'll probably need a ball, too, for the full fungo experience.

MICHAEL *(grabs a ball)*. Come on, kids. It's fungo time! *(MICHAEL goes off with a bat and ball.)*

DON *(to team)*. Lots of life out there! Assistant Coach Mike will hit you fungoes. Jimmy, you're my opening-day pitcher.

*(Sound of breaking glass. MICHAEL returns with the bat, excited.)*

MICHAEL. I need another ball. Did you see that fungo I hit?

DON. Watched it all the way. Right through my windshield.

MICHAEL. That was your van? I'm sorry. I'll pay.

DON. Forget it.

MICHAEL. No, I caused the damage, it's my responsibility.

DON. Drop it, Mike.

MICHAEL. I don't want this hanging over us all season. You resenting me for breaking your windshield—

DON. If I resent you, Mike, it won't have anything to do with the windshield.

MICHAEL. Still, I'd feel better. It's a way of teaching the team about personal responsibility.

DON. Mike, I have no problem if you want to stop talking.

MICHAEL. Tell me something. Would Tony pay for it?

DON. Hey. Don't drag Tony into this. Tony spent three years in the Phillies organization and he'd be in the majors today if he hadn't blown out his knee. He knew how to hit fungoes.

MICHAEL. I'm just going to leave money in your van. If you don't want it you can give it to a local shelter.

DON. Mike! For the love of God, we have a game to play! *(DON and MICHAEL address the team.)*

DON *(continuing).* Okay, guys, here we go! Tito, you're shortstop, because Kahil asked if he could, so Kahil, you're in centerfield. I know you'd both rather have it the other way, but that's my one rule. Go get 'em!

MICHAEL. Have fun!

DON. Which means win! "Ready position," everyone! Look at me, Timor! Ready position! Timor! *Timor! (DON demonstrates "ready position," bending forward, with hands on knees.)* Look alive out there in right field, Frankie! Rusty, you're guarding the line at third! Timmy, right foot on the bag to receive a throw! Tito, get your glove down all the way on the grounders! Eric, strong throws to second! Philip, tie those laces! Double knots! Jimmy, a little heat out on the hill!

MICHAEL *(yells to the team).* Play to the best of your ability! No one can ever ask for more than that! We're all winners if we do our best, on the playing field or at work or at home!

DON. Can I stop you, Mike? If you're going to go with that concept, don't say it like that.

MICHAEL. How should I say it?

DON. "Play within yourself."

MICHAEL. "Play within yourself"? It sounds dirty.

DON. It's not dirty. It means just play your game, don't try to play beyond your abilities.

MICHAEL. But don't we want them to try to exceed what they've already done? To strive for excellence?

DON. Yes, we do, Mike.

MICHAEL. I see our job as creating a safe and nurturing atmosphere where children can dare to be great because they aren't afraid to fail.

DON. That's not something I want you yelling from my bench.

MICHAEL. I don't feel comfortable yelling, "Play within yourself."

DON. You don't want them playing within someone else, do you?

MICHAEL. Good God, no!

DON. Just go with a different concept. More general. *(Yells.)* Let's go out there! Look alive!

MICHAEL *(yells)*. Philip! If he hits the ball to you, you *hurry*!

DON. Small point, Mike, but in baseball we don't say "hurry." We say, "go."

MICHAEL. But we want him to go fast, don't we?

DON. Or his ass will be planted on the bench.

MICHAEL. Doesn't "go fast" mean "hurry"?

DON. Technically, yes, Mike. But don't yell "hurry" because it's just plain wrong and these kids are at an impressionable age.

MICHAEL *(yells)*. Go! Go! Go!

DON. Nice chatter. But we generally don't yell that during a timeout. *(DON and MICHAEL sit on the bench. The game goes on.)* Can I point something out, Mike?

MICHAEL. Sure, anything! *(Off DON's nod toward the bleachers.)* What are we looking at?

DON. Timmy's mom.

MICHAEL. What about her?

DON. She wants me.

MICHAEL. She wants you?

DON. See what she did when I looked at her? *(DON licks his lips.)*

MICHAEL. She's eating.

DON. What rock do you live under, Mike? Wake up! There's a whole fun house out there of lonely, desperate, troubled moms. That's a major coaching perk. They see a slick guy like me and even you parading around, they can't be blamed for letting their minds run wild.

MICHAEL. Huh.

DON. I know. If I was single it would be nothing but shock and awe. *(Yells to team.)* Last inning, let's hold 'em!

MICHAEL. It's only the sixth inning.

DON. This is Little League, Mike, that's all we play.

MICHAEL. Not nine innings? Boy, everything I know is wrong. *(Yells.)* Come on, play within yourselves! *(Looks at DON.)* You're looking at your van, aren't you?

DON. No.

MICHAEL. Just so you know, you're getting the money whether you want it or not.

DON. Stop it, Mike. I mean it. *(Yells.)* Jimmy! Do not pitch until the dog is off the field!

MICHAEL. You keep looking out there, I know what you're thinking.

DON. You don't have a clue what I'm thinking.

MICHAEL. You're looking at your van.

DON. No, I am not looking at my van.

MICHAEL. You *were* looking at your van.

DON. No I wasn't.

MICHAEL. What were you looking at?

DON. I don't have to tell you what I was looking at.

MICHAEL. I know you don't have to tell me, because I know.

DON. You don't know dick. And don't look as if you know because you don't.

MICHAEL. It's pretty hard not to look as if I know because I do know.

DON. I was looking for my wife. Okay?

MICHAEL. Oh. I guess I didn't know.

DON. I thought she'd show up. Opening day.

MICHAEL. Did she say she was coming?

DON. Last year, she didn't have to say. She was just here, every inning of every game. With the best snacks, home-made health bars, the kids loved 'em. Loved the snacks, loved Linda.

MICHAEL. That's her name? Linda?

DON. You should be a private detective, the way you figure things out.

MICHAEL. Maybe she's still coming. The game's not over. And the traffic's kind of rough today...

DON. You're the only one who ever runs into traffic in this town. I don't know how the hell you find it. *(Yells.)* Nice catch, Tito! Okay, guys, two more outs and we go home! *(DON and MICHAEL watch anxiously. MI-*

*CHAEL starts making a clicking sound.)* Mike? Would you stop it?

MICHAEL. What? *(DON makes the clicking sound.)* Oh, that. It's just nerves. Sometimes it's accompanied by a rash.

DON. Don't do it anymore.

MICHAEL. It's outside my control. Ever since a childhood boating accident.

DON. No backtalk, Mike. *(Yells.)* Yes! Just one more out! Bases loaded, so you've got a play at any base! Ready position! Timor! *Timor! (They watch a fly ball to right field.)*

MICHAEL. Oh, dear God, no.

DON. Easy catch and we win, Frankie! Watch it all the way into your glove! Two hands! *(Beat.)* Damn! Well go chase it, Frankie! It's behind you!

MICHAEL. His glasses flew off. He can't see.

DON. There it is! Don't hold the ball, Frankie! Do not hold the ball in my outfield! Throw the ball!

MICHAEL. Throw the ball, Frank! Now!

DON. Don't run it in! Throw it in!

MICHAEL. Throw it to the boy who's waiting for it, like playing catch—

DON. Hit that cutoff man! *(DON explodes as the tragedy unfolds.)*

MICHAEL. It's okay to cry. Go on, let it all out...

DON. Hey! Heads held high! You're ballplayers! *(To MICHAEL.)* Jesus Christ. What a living nightmare.

MICHAEL. Except for that one play, it was a wonderful game.

DON. Excellent point, Mike. The operation would have been a total success if the patient had lived. *(Addressing the team.)* Listen up. My one rule is this: do not ever, ever, ever hold onto the ball in my outfield. Frankie, I'm talking to you. Look at me, please. Over here.

MICHAEL. We'll go to the outfield and find your glasses later, Frank. Try to look at Coach. Over here.

DON. I don't want to see anything like that again. Whatever the hell it was, it wasn't baseball.

MICHAEL. Point of order, Don. You said you wouldn't get on the kids about physical errors...

DON. That's true, Mike. What we saw here in right field today was a whole salad bar of mental errors.

MICHAEL. He missed the ball. That's a physical error.

DON. If he had used two hands, as per my instructions, he would have caught the ball. Hence, mental error.

MICHAEL. By that definition, *everything* is a mental error. Since the mind instructs the body what to do, missing a ground ball could be called a mental error.

DON. Could be and will be, for sure.

MICHAEL. So everything's mental.

DON. Pretty much. I certainly think holding onto the ball in right field and running in what looked like a figure-eight pattern while the tying and winning runs score is a huge, fat, stinking, mental error.

MICHAEL. Then why did you make this point about never yelling at 'em for physical errors if you don't think there's even any such thing as a physical error?

DON *(to the team).* Kids, Assistant Coach Mike is raising some interesting philosophical points which we can sort out in private, at a mandatory coaches' meeting. In the meantime, choke back those tears, chin up, go shake hands with the other team.

MICHAEL. Come on, Frank, let's see if we can find your glasses before the lawn mower gets them. *(MICHAEL leaves. DON gives a final look around for his wife, then leaves.)*

*(THE PARKING LOT BY THE BALLFIELD. Thunder. MICHAEL approaches DON.)*

MICHAEL. Do you really think we're going to play today?

DON. Eighty percent. The rain-outs back up on each other and it's a bitch by the ass-end of the season.

MICHAEL. I see you patched up your van.

DON. Just put cardboard over the broken windshield. It was pouring in the front like a son of a bitch.

MICHAEL. Look, I would feel better if you'd let me pay for the windshield. I don't like owing you.

DON. You don't owe me anything.

MICHAEL. I feel like I do.

DON. That's your issue, probably from childhood, something your parents did or didn't do.

MICHAEL. Are you ever going to get your windshield fixed?

DON. This isn't the time, while we're on a winning streak.

MICHAEL. You're not fixing your windshield because the team is winning?

DON. You're obviously new to the game, Mike.

MICHAEL *(re: rain)*. Think it's going to stop?

DON. It's not bad. I mean it's wet, but you have to expect that with rain.

MICHAEL. How long do we wait?

DON. Till the commissioner makes a decision. He should be here soon. He's in a work-release program.

MICHAEL. The commissioner is a criminal?

DON. That's a harsh word, Mike. He's a good commissioner, and nobody wants the job. Nobody wants to coach, either. You give up your life to get screamed at by crazy parents, half the kids resent you, it puts a huge strain on your family, and if you do it right you don't sleep at night.

MICHAEL. Then why do you coach?

DON. Why does Sinatra sing? Here's a better question. Why do you try to coach?

MICHAEL. I thought it was important to have a special activity with my son.

DON. There are other activities out there, my friend.

MICHAEL. Yes, I know. We joined Indian Guides.

DON. Sounds like fun.

MICHAEL. Does it?

DON. Was it?

MICHAEL. No. We had to go camping in the rain and call each other by our Indian names.

DON. What was your Indian name, Mike?

MICHAEL. That's not important.

DON. Yes it is. I want to know.

MICHAEL. What's important is we decided to leave the tribe and try baseball.

DON. Tell me your Indian name. Was it…Chief Itchy Itchy Scrotum?

MICHAEL. No, Don.

DON. So what was it?

MICHAEL. I'm not going to tell you.

DON. Well, until you tell me your *real* Indian name I'm going to call you Chief Itchy Itchy Scrotum.

MICHAEL. It's not a real Indian name. It's just the name we were assigned.

DON. By who?

MICHAEL. The tribal council.

DON. Sounds pretty official to me. So what name did the tribal council give you? Chief—

MICHAEL. Don't call me that. I mean it.

DON. What are you going to do? Scalp me?

MICHAEL. I'm serious. Stop it.

DON. If I said it just once in front of the kids they'd never let you forget it. Years from now, you'd be known all over town as Chief Itchy Itchy Scrotum—

MICHAEL. Don't do that. Don't say it in front of the kids.

DON. Then tell me. Chief.

MICHAEL. Look, I've had enough of that crap in my life, stupid people calling me stupid names.

DON. What was that, Mike?

MICHAEL. Nothing.

DON. You think I'm stupid because I didn't go to college and I don't have a big-ass job in the city?

MICHAEL. I don't think that.

DON. Yeah. You do think that. It just slipped out and that's what you think. You think I'm stupid.

MICHAEL. I don't think you're stupid.

DON. Then what do you think I am?

MICHAEL. I don't know.

DON. Say it. Stupid. Right?

MICHAEL. No. You're…above average.

DON. Above average? You know who else is "above average"? Everybody in the whole United States.

MICHAEL. That's not possible—

DON. Unless they're really stupid.

MICHAEL. I don't think you're really stupid.

DON. Goddamn right. I bet I can name all the states and state capitals before you. Want to try me? Huh?

MICHAEL. I don't need this right now.

DON. I'll even beat you with the provinces, you halfwit inbred Canadian bastard. You going off to pout in your wigwam?

MICHAEL. Hey! We're coaches. We should be setting an example. I thought if there was name-calling and humiliation it would be from the kids.

DON. Why should they have all the fun? Mike, baby, I'm trying to be friends, most guys would be enjoying the hell out of this.

MICHAEL. This is how you make friends?

DON. What do you want me to do, take you to the movies and snuggle? Is that how guys get acquainted in Canada?

MICHAEL. No.

DON. You're making me work too hard, Mike. You won't even tell me your Indian name. Which leaves me no choice but to call you Chief Itchy—

MICHAEL. Okay! Leaping Wolf. Okay?

DON. That's it? You were Leaping Wolf?

MICHAEL. Briefly.

DON. Why didn't you want to tell me? That's a pretty goddamn good name.

MICHAEL. You really think so?

DON. If anybody ever called me Leaping Wolf I'd put it on my driver's license and tattoo it across my ass.

MICHAEL. That's very sweet. But please don't call me that.

DON. Let's get in the van, Wolf. My wife made cookies. *(They get in DON's van. DON continuing; getting out cookies.)* Watch out for the broken glass.

MICHAEL. Do you smell something?

DON. Nah.

MICHAEL. Like an animal died in your van or something?

DON. Oh, that. *(DON holds up a foot.)*

MICHAEL. You aren't changing your socks, are you, Don?

DON. Not till they lose.

MICHAEL. So you really are pretty superstitious.

DON. No. I just don't want to jinx the team.

MICHAEL. Look, I know I'm a newcomer, but can you explain the possible connection between the activities of nine boys on a playing field and your socks?

DON. It's about faith, Mike. Believing. That's what the game is all about. Okay?

MICHAEL. I'm afraid I have to draw the line if you want me to worship your socks.

DON. That's right, take shots at me. I never had to defend myself to Tony. He understood. Once we're on a winning streak, he goes five weeks without changing his T-shirt. His girlfriend gets hammered, spills a tub of salsa on it and he can't wear it the next game. So we get bombed, 8 to 3. Thanks, Tony.

MICHAEL. I didn't know you had solid evidence to back this up.

DON. Last year was unbelievable. Tony and I would go out, plot strategy, have three or four pitchers of beer and really think outside the box. For the kids. By the end of the season we'd just sit in the dugout not saying a word. It was beautiful.

MICHAEL. If you're making a pitch for not talking, I'm okay with that.

DON. Oh, hell no, Mike, you and I don't know each other well enough to not talk.

MICHAEL. You talk to your wife?

DON. Of course! Well, not much lately, truth be told. A cold front has moved into the area. Probably from Canada, thank you very much.

MICHAEL. But the way you look at it, things must be good if you're not talking.

DON. I don't know about you, but not talking with a woman is a whole different thing from not talking to a normal person. I can't believe she hasn't come to a single game this year.

MICHAEL. Why hasn't she?

DON. She's just busy all the time. I can't keep up with where she goes, but you gotta be supportive of every whacked-out notion she dreams up: the group, the job, the volunteer community multiethnic inner-city nondenominational blah-de-blah-blah, all of which I respect. But the time gets consumed, and here we are, two guys eating cookies in a van in the rain. I haven't even met your wife. I don't even know her name.

MICHAEL. Barbara.

DON. Unbelievable.

MICHAEL. Why is that unbelievable?

DON. Six games in and I haven't even met Babs. See, it's all different. The parents last year—

MICHAEL. I bet they were pretty amazing.

DON. How did you know?

MICHAEL. Lucky guess.

DON. You know what they would do at the games? The Wave. Now, personally, I hate that crap, but it worked, it got the kids jazzed. And afterwards, me and Tony and Linda would go out and drink beers. I know you don't drink beer, you have your reasons, not a criticism, I'm just saying we'd have some laughs after the games. Tony was going through a nasty breakup, his girlfriend Trish didn't necessarily kill his dog but was a possible accessory. She had mental problems, a disease, not her fault, I don't judge. Maybe one night after the game you and Babs and me could go, not for beer, but what does she like, wine coolers?

MICHAEL. Is that the commissioner with the thing on his ankle?

DON *(gets out of the van)*. It's stopped raining! Let's play two! *(Calling.)* C'mon, team! Out of the cars and onto the field!

MICHAEL. I'll hit fungoes! Carefully!

*(THE BALLFIELD. DON is coaching first base.)*

DON *(calls to Frankie, the batter)*. Start something going, Frank. You're the man! Big hitter! Get ready up there! Look at me! *(Demonstrates correct batting stance.)* Step into the ball. You're bailing out on every pitch. Like this. Like you're scared. *(Demonstrates Frank's awkward stance, aimed at getting out of the way of the pitch.)* Don't worry, he's not going to hit you! *(Recoils as if hit.)* Ouch! Bad luck! You're okay, Frank, that's what the helmet is for. How to take one for the team. Now pick yourself up and come on down to first base. *(To Frank, now the runner at first base.)* Shake it off,

Frankie, a slight ringing sensation in your ears is per-
fectly natural. One out, you have to run if it's on the
ground. *(Calls to batter.)* Wait for your pitch and drive
it, Kahil! Elbow up, look at me! *(DON demonstrates his
batting stance for Kahil.)* Now look to me for the signal
*before* you get in the batters' box! *(DON does a compli-
cated series of signals, looks at Kahil, does the signals
again, more slowly, then calls:)* Hit away! *(To the runner.)* You're the tying run, Frank, look alive. Wait till
the end of the inning if you have to cry. *(To the batter.)*
Guard that plate, Kahil, keep the rally going! *Yes! (To
runner.)* Go, Frank, it's going to drop, he doesn't have a
chance! Run, Frankie, run! *(Beat.)* Shoot! Get back,
Frank! Now! Back! Don't get doubled up! He caught it,
the lucky little so and so! My fault... *(The game ends.
DON, defeated, slumps on the bench.)*

MICHAEL. Don? When you were coaching first, do you
think that was a mental or a physical error? Since you
weren't even on the field, it couldn't have been physical,
so it must have been mental, right?

DON. Shut up, Mike. I exercised poor judgment. I let the
team down.

MICHAEL. Come on, our first loss since opening day. And
everyone played great. Except for you...and you didn't
even play.

DON. What the hell is wrong with you?

MICHAEL. I'm trying to be a friend and cheer you up.

DON. Well, stop it! What kind of man are you? Losing
doesn't even bother you.

MICHAEL. The game is over. Everybody did their best.
Now families are congratulating their kids, maybe taking
them for ice cream. Two other teams are getting ready to

play, full of hope. Win or lose, it's a pretty nice afternoon in the park.

DON. Tell me something. Why are you here?

MICHAEL. What?

DON. I want to know why you're here. Making fun of me and making fun of the game of baseball.

MICHAEL. I'm not making fun of you. I guess I'm just glad to be a part of this. I was the kid who never got picked to play, who ended up always watching. I don't want Frankie to be the kid who never gets picked. That's why I'm here.

DON. Well, I hope this is a rich and fulfilling experience for both of you.

MICHAEL. You don't own baseball, Don. So let me and my kid have just a little piece of it for ourselves, okay? *(Putting equipment away.)* Hey, have you seen the other shin guard?

DON. No.

MICHAEL. It's gotta be here someplace.

DON. Unless Eric wore it home by accident. Kids will make you crazy with the whacked-out stuff they pull. *(DON finds the shin guard.)* Here it is.

MICHAEL. Oh, good. Thanks.

DON *(holds onto it)*. That doesn't mean you stop looking.

MICHAEL. What?

DON. I'm the one who found it. And it was your responsibility. So you have to keep looking.

MICHAEL. How am I supposed to find it?

DON. I can guarantee you won't find it if you don't look.

MICHAEL. Where do you want me to look?

DON. Just around. I'm sure it'll turn up someplace. *(MICHAEL goes through the motions of looking.)* Any luck?

MICHAEL. Not yet. *(DON tosses the shin guard on the ground. MICHAEL gets it.)* Oh. Here it is. I found it.

DON. Nice going. *(Watches MICHAEL put the shin guard in the bag.)* Man, I feel like I'm all alone this year.

MICHAEL. What do you mean?

DON. Tony would have enjoyed the hell out of that, having to look for a shin guard I already found.

MICHAEL. I enjoyed it.

DON. Did you, Mike?

MICHAEL. Yes I did. Big-time.

DON. Honestly? Because I couldn't tell.

MICHAEL. It was more of an inner enjoyment.

DON. There you go. You wouldn't even share your enjoyment. So I have to come up with hilarious stuff like making you look for the shin guard *and* I have to enjoy it enough for the both of us. I do it all. You know who besides me has brought snacks? Answer? Nobody.

MICHAEL. I didn't know you were bringing all the snacks.

DON. Well now you do. Snacks are an integral part of the Little League experience. How come *you* never bring snacks, Mike? I can accept I won't ever hear any brilliant game strategy from you, but how about a word across the pillow to Babs that a little contribution would be much appreciated? Huh?

MICHAEL. The name is Barbara.

DON. It she doesn't want to come to a single game, fine. I don't judge someone else's lack of support for their own child. But Babs could get down off her high horse and stop at the Food Emporium and buy some worthless crap to show the kids we care—

MICHAEL. My wife is dead, Don.

DON. What?

MICHAEL. Barbara. My wife. She's dead. So she won't be bringing any worthless crap for the kids.

DON. What are you saying? When did this happen?

MICHAEL. A year ago.

DON. Babs is dead? I never even got a chance to meet her.

MICHAEL. The name is Barbara. I'll bring snacks next game. I didn't know I was supposed to.

DON. Jesus Christ, Mikey.

MICHAEL. And while we're on it, don't call me Mikey. Or Mike. My name is Michael. Is that asking a lot to want to get called by my own name?

DON. Why didn't you ever tell me about your wife?

MICHAEL. I didn't want to talk about it. I just wanted to be the assistant coach.

DON. So you let me ramble on like some kind of a five-star asshole, how we should all get together for wine coolers and why doesn't she bring snacks…

MICHAEL. It's okay.

DON. Yeah, sure, it's okay for *you*, but what about me? I feel like a jerk. See, Mikey, Mike, *Michael*, you keep it all bottled up inside, creating a ball of stress that will just build and build and one day explode and kill you, but that's not my business, I don't judge. The question is, how am I supposed to know who's sitting next to me on the bench?

MICHAEL. I told you, didn't I?

DON. Sure, it only took seven games.

MICHAEL. About the only time I don't think about her is when I'm here. I'm tired, Don, I needed a break.

DON. So where is Frankie's father?

MICHAEL. Nepal.

DON. Nepal? The one in...Nepal?

MICHAEL. That's the one. He's been on a pilgrimage for seven years now.

DON. I'd like to take a goddamn pilgrimage. Where do I sign up for my pilgrimage?

MICHAEL. So in answer to your question, I'm Frankie's father.

DON. Good for you. Frankie's a smart kid.

MICHAEL. Why do you say that?

DON. He just seems smart.

MICHAEL. Why? Because he never understands the drills the first time? Because he still doesn't know what a cutoff man is?

DON. I don't know, he seems smart. Maybe it's the glasses and the way he's always so out of it. I just don't get why everything's a big mystery with you. Your dead wife, your kid's father, your Indian name—

MICHAEL. Can I ask you something? How come you never make Frank stay after practice?

DON. You said that was punishment. You thought the kids should run off and be captains of their little ships.

MICHAEL. I just would like him to be better friends with the other kids on the team.

DON. If Frankie ever caught a fly ball or got a hit it would sure help make his bones.

MICHAEL. That's why he needs extra practice. I hate to see Eric get all the breaks because of his eye-twitch.

DON. Michael, I got twelve kids on my team and no one to help me teach the fundamentals.

MICHAEL. Then why don't you ask Tony to come back and coach?

DON. I would, but his kid's in Babe Ruth League and Tony's coaching. He makes fun of the guys who stick around coaching after their kids move on, the Get-a-Lifers. So now I never see him. My goddamn best friend. Everyone's so busy and you never see the people you care about and your time gets sucked up by people who don't matter. *(Watching MICHAEL struggle with the equipment.)* Could I make a small, supportive suggestion relating to the equipment?

MICHAEL *(turning on him).* I've got it, Don. So why don't you give me a break and leave?

DON. What's your problem?

MICHAEL. You. You're my problem.

DON. I didn't do anything. What did I do?

MICHAEL. Maybe it's nothing you did. Maybe it's just who you are.

DON. You think it's easy being me? I'd like to see you try it, you wouldn't get through the first ten minutes of my day. My wife would scramble you up and eat you for breakfast with a side of sausage if you were me. I know every angle and it's all I can do to hold the line. So how about a little goddamn compassion, Michael, if that word is even in your vocabulary.

MICHAEL. Fine. And how about you stop torturing me. I thought this was supposed to be fun.

DON. Where did you hear that? This isn't supposed to be fun.

MICHAEL. Then why are we here?

DON. Jesus Christ! Look, Michael, in your candy-ass world you hand out Popsicles and tell all the kids they're great and nobody should ever feel bad. Now that's a helluva world but it isn't the real world. In the real world everything's hard. Jobs are hard, money's hard, being alone's hard, being with someone else is impossible. Ever notice who the happy people are? Winners. Everyone else is thirty seconds away from blowing their goddamn brains out. You want to give these kids something? Make 'em winners. Give 'em a shot at a life that doesn't break their heart. That's the hardest thing you'll ever do, which you'd know if you made a real commitment.

MICHAEL. I made a commitment!

DON. Did you, Michael?

MICHAEL. Yes, I did! *(MICHAEL's cell phone rings. They stare at each other as it rings.)* I actually have to take this.

DON. Some kind of commitment, big-shot.

*(MICHAEL answers the phone as LIGHTS FADE TO BLACK.)*

## END OF ACT I

# ACT II

*(THE BALLFIELD. MICHAEL addresses the team.)*

MICHAEL. I guess we'd better get started. Since Coach Don isn't here, I guess I'm in charge. Just for today, let's try something different. All of you play the position you want to play, how does that sound? *(Beat.)* Hey! Take it easy, you can't *all* be shortstop! Give me a minute, I'll figure something out here. Maybe we'll rotate, so everyone gets a chance...

*(DON enters.)*

MICHAEL *(continuing)*. Look who's here! We'd about given up on you, Coach Don!
DON. My one rule about tardiness—everyone can be late *once.*
MICHAEL. Where's Jimmy?
DON. Today, we're going to give more of you a chance to pitch. Rusty, I can't help but think if you harness all your many pounds to a fastball, you'd be an object of terror on the mound.
MICHAEL. Jimmy didn't hurt his arm, did he?
DON. Nah, Jimmy's arm is perfect. Unfortunately, Jimmy's head is a different story.

MICHAEL. Is he all right?

DON *(to the team).* Some of you heard the rumors at school. Sadly, it's true. Jimmy's gone and got himself a part in *Brigadoon.*

MICHAEL. Thank God he's okay.

DON. Jimmy apparently feels his talents are best used in service to the American musical theater. He wanted me to read this. *(Gets out paper.)* "It's with deep regret that I've decided to leave the team. I'll miss my teammates, the fans, who've always been great to me, and the entire organization. At this point in my life, I'm looking forward to a new challenge, and the chance to spend more time with my family." *(Beat.)* There's a proud tradition in baseball of rising above tragedy. I hope you kids will do just that and win another championship. Now grab a ball and start warming up! *(DON sits on the bench, depressed.)*

MICHAEL. I had no idea Jimmy was a song and dance man.

DON. You think you know your own kid and then... whack! You get hit in the face with a two-by-four.

MICHAEL. You know, Frankie went through this stage of wearing his mother's shoes and scarfs and belting out old Motown songs in front of the mirror: "Stop! In the name of love!"

DON. Is this supposed to make me feel better?

MICHAEL. The point is this: When Barbara and I finally accepted that this little whirling diva was Frankie, he announced he was going out for soccer and that was it for the Supremes.

DON. Interesting personal anecdote, Michael. Much appreciated. Jimmy hasn't sunk to the dress stage yet, but this sure as hell is a wake-up call. Here I am, trying to brace myself for when he knocks up a girl or gets busted for dope and he goes and pulls this *Brigadoon* nightmare out of his ass. Who could have seen this one coming?

MICHAEL. Don't blame yourself. These kids, they're strange and inscrutable beasts.

DON. We had it out last night. He wouldn't cave in like he usually does. Has his heart set on the school play.

MICHAEL. So why were you late?

DON. Michael, I did something I'm not proud of.

MICHAEL. What did you do?

DON. I offered him money to play ball.

MICHAEL. Really? How much?

DON. Jesus Christ, does it matter how much? *(Beat.)* Twenty bucks a game.

MICHAEL. Wow. We have, what, six games left plus the playoffs, times twenty—

DON. Hey, it's his identity, his future, it's who he is. I was an athlete, that's how everyone knew me. It got me out of final exams and into bed with girls. It got me through the endless crap they throw in your way to try to break you down and kill you. How can you put a price on that?

MICHAEL. So what did he say?

DON. He wanted fifty a game.

MICHAEL. I guess Jimmy could put a price on it.

DON. That was right when Linda got home. She was so understanding toward Jimmy: "We all have to follow what's in our heart," I could have... *(Clenches fist.)* not that I ever would...

MICHAEL. No, of course not.

DON. Because that's a disease that affects rich and poor alike, and it means everybody has to run off to shelters and get lots of professional help. Bottom line? Jimmy's gone over to the other side.

MICHAEL. That's quite a blow to the team. I guess everyone will have to work just a little harder.

DON. That's right, Michael, starting at the very top. Things are going to be different around here. You might want to write this down. One. From now on, you have to be on time unless you notify me twenty-four hours in advance. Two. You have to be authentically upset when we lose. Three. You're not allowed to tell the kids to "have fun" except as it relates to winning. And four, you're not allowed to cheer me up, because it always brings me down. Think you can do this?

MICHAEL. If that's the way you want it, Don.

DON. Let's go find us a pitcher.

*(THE BALLFIELD, another game. DON is cheering the team on.)*

DON. Big stick up there, Timmy! You're the man, Tim-bo! Look at me, Tim-ster, walk's as good as a hit! Timmy-Timmy-Timmy, good eye, take your base, Timmy-Tim!

MICHAEL. You're really on the Timmy bandwagon today.

DON. Little thing called quid pro quo.

MICHAEL. What do you mean?

DON. Me and Mrs. Timmy.

MICHAEL. Really?

DON. Parents' Night at the middle school. My wife had the flu and the ex-Mr. Timmy's currently in jail—

MICHAEL. Actually he's living in the city—

DON. Same difference. So me and Mrs. Timmy are going class to class talking about standardized testing. Next thing I know we're hunkered down in her Subaru in the darkest part of the parking lot. *(Yells.)* Two out, Timmy, run on anything!

MICHAEL. What happened?

DON. What do you think happened, Michael? *(Yells.)* No leading, Tim-ster!

MICHAEL. That's a lousy thing, Don.

DON. What?

MICHAEL. You're married.

DON. What's your point?

MICHAEL. You shouldn't be doing that.

DON. You think I don't know that? I'm only human and so is Mrs. Timmy. I just can't help thinking if my wife took better care of herself she never would have got the flu and put me in that position with Mrs. Timmy. *(Yells.)* Aw, what are you swinging at, Rusty? Run to your positions! Show some character! *(To MICHAEL.)* How'd you know Mrs. Timmy's ex is in the city?

MICHAEL. She told me.

DON. You talk to her?

MICHAEL. She helps me put the equipment in my car sometimes.

DON. Huh. You're in sweet shape, my friend. You got a desperate woman holding on for dear life, plus a dead wife, which is money in the bank. Man, you're living my dream.

*(THE BALLFIELD. Practice. DON is addressing the team.)*

DON. I just want to say I am so proud of you kids. Granted, you're not the most talented players I've ever seen. You drop fly balls, you throw wildly, you strike out, and I don't remember another team at any level that cries as much as this one. Frankly, you don't match up against the elite teams in our league. But you showed me something. You rose to the challenge. You made friends with adversity. You got into the playoffs. Nice work.

*(MICHAEL enters with the duffel bag.)*

MICHAEL. Quick question, Coach Don. Don't *all* the teams get in the playoffs?

DON. Yes, they do, Assistant Coach Michael. But let's not let that detract from what these young men have accomplished. Incidentally, you're in violation of our first condition, relating to punctuality.

MICHAEL. I let you know twenty-four hours in advance.

DON. No you didn't, but we'll take this up in a special coaches' meeting after practice. *(To the team.)* How do we succeed in the playoffs? Answer: by winning games. How do we win games? Answer: by scoring more runs than the other team. That's why we're instituting some new and exciting strategy for the playoffs. *(Motioning them closer.)* Everyone around me. This is so top secret I don't even want you telling your parents. Can I trust you? *(Beat.)* Pay attention—over here, Frankie. This is our new signal. *(DON turns his baseball cap around backwards.)* Pretty easy to spot, even without your glasses. What does it mean? As soon as you get on base, you look at me. If my hat is turned around like this, when you get to the next base, you *slide*. And when you slide, pretend to injure your leg. Hold onto it, yell, squirt a few tears. That shouldn't be a stretch for most of you. Why do I want you to do this? So we can take you out of the game and put in a faster runner and maybe get a run we wouldn't have scored otherwise. This is a special signal for our slower runners. Rusty would be an excellent candidate. Frankie, if lightning strikes and you find yourself on first base, by all means, wipe off your glasses and check my hat.

MICHAEL. That isn't strategy. That's called cheating.

DON. Assistant Coach Michael, because of your many years of inexperience, you're in no position to debate the finer points of the game with the likes of me.

MICHAEL. This isn't about baseball, this is about right and wrong. I will not be a part of this.

DON. That's your decision, and I accept it. You can go sit quietly in your car till we're done.

MICHAEL. I'm not leaving practice, if that's what you're thinking.

DON. I'm thinking I cannot allow you to take shots at my strategy and confuse my team.

MICHAEL. It's my team, too, and I don't want them to cheat. If we can't find a way to win fair and square, then I, personally, would rather lose.

DON. You can't stand up in front of people in their formative years and say you would prefer to lose.

MICHAEL. I would prefer to lose than cheat.

DON. Please don't waste our time quoting from the Handbook of Curling. This is baseball.

MICHAEL. This is wrong.

DON *(to the team)*. Team? Why don't we start by taking a lap around the field. I've decided to move up the coaches' meeting to an earlier time. *(To MICHAEL.)* We have lost our best player. I feel responsible that it is my kid putting on makeup and prancing about in tights instead of whiffing guys with his fastball. I lie awake nights thinking about how we can make up for that terrible gaping hole in our lineup. I owe this to the kids.

MICHAEL. Let them play, Don. Just let them play. It's okay.

DON. That's very impressive strategy. "Just let them play." Did you come up with that while you were the only car stuck in traffic?

MICHAEL. Let me ask you something. What do you think the commissioner would have to say about this?

DON. Our commissioner was convicted of transporting cigarettes over state lines for the purpose of illegal sale. So I can't imagine my Little League game strategy will put his panties in a twirl. Now let me ask you something about dedication and commitment. Do you ever think about the team when you aren't actually here?

MICHAEL. Yes, I do.

DON. How much?

MICHAEL. A lot.

DON. Waking hours, what percentage?

MICHAEL. What percentage of my waking hours do I spend thinking about the team?

DON. I would say with me it's fifty-five percent. Easy. Then I think about money maybe twenty-five percent of the time. And the rest is all sex and revenge fantasies. You honestly don't know your percentages?

MICHAEL. I haven't stopped to figure it out, Don.

DON. Gee, a bright, successful big-shot like you, and you never even stopped to think about what you think about? And then you come here to the field where I have coached my heart out for the last seven years and stab me in the back in front of my team. Ever read the rule book, Michael?

MICHAEL. No.

DON. 'Course not. Because it might get in the way of your half-ass opinions. Well, you should know that my new strategy is fully sanctioned by the official Little League rule book. Injured runners may be replaced.

MICHAEL. But they're not really injured. They're just *acting* injured.

DON. *Acting?* Was that a shot at Jimmy?

MICHAEL. No, it was a shot at you. For getting so carried away with winning you'd teach these kids to cheat.

DON. Fact: you serve here at my discretion. If I say the word you're an ex-assistant coach and I am so close to saying the word I can taste it.

MICHAEL. You know I'm right.

DON. I know there's no place for you in baseball. A man who doesn't care if he wins, who has nothing to teach his son except the finer points of being a loser.

MICHAEL. Don't call me a loser. And don't drag my son into this.

DON. Fine. Then don't you mention Jimmy.

MICHAEL. I won't.

DON. Because Jimmy is the best player on the team.

MICHAEL. Except he isn't on the team.

DON. I'm warning you, Michael. You've been no help to me this season. I've had to do everything: schedules, snacks, fungoes.

MICHAEL. You're still angry I broke the window of your van.

DON. I wasn't talking about that.

MICHAEL. I offered to pay and you wouldn't let me. You wanted to hold it over me.

DON. Let's be honest here, Michael. We both know why you kept offering to pay.

MICHAEL. Because I felt responsible.

DON. You couldn't cut it as coach so you had to fling your money in my face. You and your big-shot company.

MICHAEL. What are you talking about?

DON. Your company, Michael, couldn't wait to tell me you had your own company—

MICHAEL. It isn't my company.

DON. Oh, really? Then we can add "liar" to your rap sheet. I know for a fact you shot off your mouth about "my company" with the "government contracts."

MICHAEL. I meant the company where I work. My company. "My company has offices in Japan…"

DON. I frankly don't care where the hell your company has offices, Michael—

MICHAEL. I'm giving an example of how I meant it was just a company I work for. Not *my* company.

DON. Okay, deeply misleading, but I accept that. The point is, you wanted to pay for my windshield to show you were the one with the high-dollar job while I'm just a jerk with a van—

MICHAEL. Don, again, you're so deeply wrong.

DON. I have stood right here countless times with my clipboard while you take phone calls that you think are more important than the kids.

MICHAEL. I take those calls from my boss. Roger. A twenty-four-year-old guy who likes to order me around. I used to have an okay job but I got busted down to being Roger's assistant because I missed so much work.

DON. Tardy? Stuck in unbelievable traffic?

MICHAEL. I missed a lot of work when my wife was sick.

DON. Boy, you just can't wait to play that trump card, can you?

MICHAEL. And I was late today because I had to make sure Roger's new office furniture arrived. I don't think that's what a big-shot would be doing.

DON. It wouldn't be a problem. All you had to do is call.

MICHAEL. I did call.

DON. You didn't talk to me.

MICHAEL. I talked to Linda. Your wife.

DON. Linda, my wife? Nice try. Linda was at a school board meeting that went late. She didn't even get home till eleven-thirty.

MICHAEL. I called at seven-thirty.

DON. Did you tell her you'd be late for practice?

MICHAEL. She said she was on the other line and she'd get back to me.

DON. Yeah? And did she?

MICHAEL. What happened was she got back on my line but she must have thought she was still on the other line.

DON. Why do you think that?

MICHAEL. She said, "I'll meet you at the usual place."

DON. Who was she talking to?

MICHAEL. Beats me. I was on my line, she was on hers.

DON. She must have said a name.

MICHAEL. Nope.

DON. You're a terrible liar.

MICHAEL. That's not true. My wife used to think I was a pretty darn good liar.

DON. So you're lying?

MICHAEL. No, she really thought I was a good liar.

DON. Are you lying about this person my wife said she'd meet?

MICHAEL. That part is all true.

DON. Okay. So tell me the name she used.

MICHAEL. Think about it, Don, she wouldn't necessarily use a name.

DON. But she *did* use a name, didn't she? *(Beat.)* Give me the name, Michael. Or there's going to be some serious trouble here at the George "Bucky" Philips Community Park.

MICHAEL. Look, the kids are coming back.

DON *(yells to team).* Hey! Take another lap! *(Beat.)* Because conditioning is important for the playoffs! You want to be champions? *(DON turns back to MICHAEL, who's put on a catcher's mask.)* What the hell are you doing, Michael?

MICHAEL. Are we going to have a fistfight?

DON. Of course not, pal. Take off the mask. *(MICHAEL takes off the mask.)* And tell me what Linda said.

MICHAEL. What if I don't tell you?

DON *(grabs a bat).* I'll kill you. But rest assured, we won't fight. *(DON puts MICHAEL in a choke hold.)*

MICHAEL. Stop, please! You said we wouldn't fight!

DON. Don't fight back, then we won't be fighting. *(Holds tighter, choking him.)* The one thing you need to know is, I will do this. I will choke the life right out of you. What did she say?

MICHAEL. She said...I'll meet you at the usual place, Tee-Bee.

DON. Tee-Bee?

MICHAEL. I don't know. It sounded like that.

DON. Tee-Bee. Tony Barone. *(Lets MICHAEL go.)* I never wanted to get call waiting.

MICHAEL. I agree. People will always call back if it's important. *(Beat.)* I'm sure there's an explanation.

DON. Of course there is. A damn good explanation.

MICHAEL. There you go! *(Beat.)* What do you think it is?

DON. Either they were planning a surprise party for me, or my wife's banging my best friend.

MICHAEL. Boy, wouldn't it be great if it was a surprise party? *(Beat.)* Don?

DON. Before you talk, remember you're strictly prohibited from cheering me up. Still want to talk?

MICHAEL. No.

DON *(explodes)*. GODDAMMIT! *(Re: clipboard.)* How would you like to have a look?

MICHAEL. You mean it? I can't believe you're actually letting me look at the clipboard.

DON. Stats on each kid, my analysis of their progress, game by game. You'll find general team philosophy. Bullet points of pre-game speeches, amusing and inspirational anecdotes. School or family pressures we should be aware of.

MICHAEL. What's going on, Don?

DON. I think it's time to drop the "assistant" from your job description.

MICHAEL. You can't quit.

DON. How can I stay? Oh, you'll need this, too. *(DON tosses MICHAEL the whistle and exits.)*

MICHAEL *(blows whistle to the team)*. I know it's hot out here and that was a long run, so it anyone feels faint you can sit down. Huh. Everyone feels faint. Coach Don had to leave early, so I'm pretty much the coach. For now. *(Glances at clipboard.)* As we move into the playoffs, I'd like to share an amusing anecdote. When former assistant coach Tony was in the Phillies organization... you know, I'll table that particular anecdote. Instead, let's just do what you guys want to do. Play ball. Count off, one, two, one, two, the ones play...the twos.

*(OUTSKIRTS OF TOWN. Dusk. DON gets out of his van brushing his teeth. MICHAEL enters.)*

MICHAEL. Don?

DON. Oh, hey, Michael.

MICHAEL. How's it going?

DON. Great. Really great.

MICHAEL. Is it okay I dropped by like this?

DON. I guess it'll have to be.

MICHAEL. I've seen your van around town. The other night, out by the quarry, I was going to visit. But your light was off so I thought you might be asleep.

DON. What are you saying, Michael?

MICHAEL. I'm not saying anything.

DON. You're saying something.

MICHAEL. No, I'm just saying.

DON. What?

MICHAEL. Nothing.

DON. Sure you're not. Wink wink.

MICHAEL. Wink wink what?

DON. Wink wink I'm living in my van, that's what you're saying. But it isn't true.

MICHAEL. But your van's parked in different locations around town every night. You have all your clothes in back. And you were just brushing your teeth.

DON. I brush at regular intervals throughout the day. It calms me down and keeps my teeth clean and shiny. What do you want, Michael?

MICHAEL. I thought you should know what happened in our first playoff game. It was tied in the last inning and Rusty was on first and I got so nervous I was making that clicking sound and I turned my hat around backwards, not even thinking. Rusty saw it and ran to second and slid in and started crying. So I helped him off the field and put in Timor who stole third and then home and we won. After the game I asked Rusty if he was okay and he said, "Duh. You gave me the hurt sign, Coach." *(Hands DON clipboard.)* You want to see the stats?

DON *(examines clipboard).* You've invented some strange symbols for scoring a game. But overall, it looks not totally bad. So my substitute runner strategy worked?

MICHAEL. By accident.

DON. Glad to help out.

MICHAEL. Plus the personal stuff you have about each kid? It really helped, knowing their family situation. The divorces, the bankruptcies, the transgender issues.

DON. Hey, that's just what the job is.

MICHAEL. What you wrote about Frank—how he's learning what it is to be on a team, even though his father should have exposed him to it sooner—

DON. Hey. My one rule about clipboards. You read 'em, you don't discuss 'em, Michael.

MICHAEL. Oh, one other thing. If it's not too much trouble, could you please call me "Mike"?

DON. I thought you didn't like that.

MICHAEL. I didn't at first. No one ever called me "Mike" before. But I kind of miss being "Mike."

DON. Doesn't matter, since I have no reason to see you anymore.

MICHAEL. But if we ever ran into each other, say, at the Food Emporium, you could say, "Hey, Mike, how's it going?"

DON. Finally, something to look forward to.

MICHAEL. If you need a place to stay or take a shower, I mean if you ever did find yourself living in your van—

DON. Mikey, I'll be honest with you.

MICHAEL. Oh, while we're on it, I'm not all that crazy about "Mikey." Can we stay with "Mike"?

DON. Jesus Christ.

MICHAEL. You're right. Good point. Sorry.

DON. What I'm saying, is, the van, the questions, forget it. Linda and I are going to work it out.

MICHAEL. Good for you!

DON. We all screw up, maybe there were times when I was doing stuff with people, women-people, that technically I shouldn't have been doing, but the point is, we need to forgive each other and ourselves and not let a few mistakes ruin our lives. So we're giving it another shot.

MICHAEL. I am really glad to hear that, Don.

DON. Yeah, thanks. I haven't run it by her yet, but it sounds pretty good, doesn't it?

MICHAEL. I buy it. Good luck.

DON. You too. Hope you win that championship game.

MICHAEL. It's been a great season, win or lose.

DON. That's the idea. No pressure, play it like it's just another game.

*(THE BALLFIELD. MICHAEL does stretching exercises before the playoff game.)*

MICHAEL. Come on, you guys, no pressure. It's just another game. No reason to be nervous.

*(MICHAEL starts doing the Macarena. DON enters with a box of snacks.)*

DON. I knew you knew the Macarena!

MICHAEL. Oh, hey, Don. Just trying to loosen up the team. What are you doing here?

DON. I brought snacks. Linda's homemade health bars.

MICHAEL. Great. Thanks. *(Beat.)* You going to stick around?

DON. No, no way. I got stuff I gotta do.

MICHAEL. Right.

DON. I went to see that *Brigadoon* thing last night. Let me tell you, Jimmy kicked their asses, especially on the dance numbers. If they'd been keeping score he would have won easy.

MICHAEL. Nice. We could sure use him here.

DON. What are you gonna do?

MICHAEL. Hey, last game, you feel like coaching first base?

DON. Okay. I mean if you need the help.

MICHAEL *(to the team)*. Hey, kids, Coach Don is going to help me out today. Isn't that great? *(To DON.)* I'm not taking any chances. I haven't changed my underwear since the playoffs started.

DON. You're becoming a real baseball man, Mike.

MICHAEL. I have a confession to make, Don.

DON. Oh? What's that?

MICHAEL. I really want to win.

DON. You're in the championship. You're already a winner.

MICHAEL. No, I know it's just another game and everything but I'm telling you, I really want to win.

DON. Hey, keep the kids relaxed and focused and who knows?

MICHAEL. No, you don't understand. I really really want to win.

DON. Sometimes it's just a matter of which way the ball bounces.

MICHAEL. Easy for you to say. You have a basement—or van—full of trophies. I've never won anything, ever. Neither has Frankie. This is our one chance. *(MICHAEL's phone rings.)* Oh, shoot! Roger must have found out we had a big game and he's going to wreck it. Damn! *(DON takes the ringing phone from MICHAEL.)* What are you doing, Don?

DON. You're a winner, Mike. Winners aren't at the beck and call of every lame bastard who has them on speed dial. *(DON grabs a bat.)*

MICHAEL. Don't do this, Don. This is my very job.

DON. Your boss isn't your boss, Mike. Who's your boss?

MICHAEL. I know I'm supposed to say "me" but I'm not sure that's totally true in this case.

DON. All you gotta do is believe it. Come on, Mikey, are you the boss?

MICHAEL. Okay.

DON. That's the spirit! Listen to this goddamn thing. You can tell the guy's a prick just from the ring. I do this for you. *(DON smashes the bat down on the ringing phone. It stops ringing.)*

MICHAEL. You did it.

DON. Oh, yeah. Not the first time, either.

MICHAEL. Thanks, Don.

DON. Hey, no sweat. It had to be done.

MICHAEL. You know what? I feel good. I feel very good. I stood up to him. With your help, of course. *(To the smashed phone.)* Take that, Roger! *I'm* the boss today! You...prick!

DON. Feels good to take charge of your life, doesn't it?

MICHAEL. Yes, it does. I've got to start doing more of that. I feel really good. I think I'd feel even better if it wasn't my mother calling.

DON. You knew it was your mother? Why didn't you tell me?

MICHAEL. Because then you wouldn't have smashed my phone. Now we can concentrate on baseball. *(Yells.)* Ready position, Timor! *Timor! (MICHAEL demonstrates "ready position.")* Talk it up out there! I can't hear you! Philip, you've *got* to tie those shoelaces! That's why you tripped! *(To DON.)* Shoelaces have been a team problem all season.

DON. It's a problem every season.

MICHAEL. I don't know what they have against double knots! It's shameful!

DON. Easy, Mike. Stay in the game. *(They anxiously watch the game.)*

MICHAEL. Don?

DON. Yes, Mike?

MICHAEL. I think I'm going to make that clicking sound you hate.

DON. Oh, man. Do you have to?

MICHAEL. Yes, I do.

DON. I'm not happy about it. But click away. *(DON silently endures MICHAEL's clicking sound.)* Hey, you know who's looking good?

MICHAEL. Eric? He's playing the game of his life.

DON *(nods to bleachers)*. Mrs. Timmy. Same blouse she wore to Parents' Night. Plus, she smiled at me. I should take a run at her now that I'm living in my van.

MICHAEL. Yeah, women can't resist that.

DON. What...you don't think she'd go out with me?

MICHAEL. Actually, Don, I kind of made a date with her.

DON. You? With Mrs. Timmy?

MICHAEL. Carolyn.

DON. Oh, *Carolyn*. Must be serious if you know her name. *(Beat.)* That's good, Mike. I've been very worried about you, the way you come across like such a nothing sometimes, but this is excellent. I'm very happy for you.

MICHAEL. Is it really okay, Don? Because the two of you *did* spend time in her Subaru.

DON. And you know what happened? Nothing. I just couldn't.

MICHAEL. Huh.

DON *(jumps up)*. Great play, Eric! Major league caliber! *(Yells to one of the parents watching.)* Hey, why don't you tell your son he made a great play, huh? *(Beat.)* Come on, you're louder than that whenever he screws up! I don't think he heard you! I want to hear you say, "Great play, Eric!" *(Beat.)* This *is* my business, pal! And I'd be glad to discuss it with you in the parking lot, you dumb dirtbag son of a bitch! *(DON starts for Eric's dad and MICHAEL pulls him back to the bench.)*

MICHAEL. I need you here, Don. He's not worth it. *(To team in field.)* Timor! You'd have stopped it if you were in ready position! *(To DON.)* How many millions of times have we told him that? *(To the team.)* Two outs, play at any base! Bear down and get this out! *(Watching the action.)* Oh, no.

DON *(watching the action).* Boy oh boy. He clocked it. *(Looking toward right field, calls.)* You got it, Frankie, it's all yours!

MICHAEL. Dear God, please let him catch this ball. Just this once, let him know what it feels like to have the ball stay in his glove and not go bouncing past so he chases it in a mad terror with everyone screaming and when he finally finds it he has no idea what to do. We've done that. Many times. Let him catch this ball. Let him have this one memory for the rest of his life, that summer afternoon when the ball fell into his glove and stayed there. And let him jog back to the bench smiling in spite of himself, getting pats on the back from his teammates, still clutching the ball that didn't get away. He's never had that and he may never have the chance again. Check your stats, God, he's twelve years old, his first and last year of Little League, no team for my boy next year. So this is it. Now, God, if you're really there—and for the purposes of right now, I'm assuming you are—this is a pretty small request. Last year I asked you to let my wife live, and yes, that was a big one and I know you had your reasons for what happened, which I try to respect although I will never understand. But this should be a no-brainer. The bases are loaded, the score is tied, it's the fifth inning, Frankie has already struck out three times plus a ball got past him in right field and went all the way to the fence—a bad hop, not his fault, just one more example of your peculiar sense of humor which has caused so much hilarity through the ages. I guess what I'm trying to tell you is this: I need to feel hope. I want to believe there's a purpose to all this. That somewhere there's some meaning to the dropped fly balls and the endless hours in the hospital waiting room and the daily dread of getting out of bed. I don't need much, but I need something—a hint, a sign, a quick "thumbs-up" from the Home Office. Just once, I need this boy to catch the ball. Please.

DON. Nice catch, Frankie!

MICHAEL *(to God)*. Thank you.

DON. Frankie's doing a helluva job handling the high-fives for a first-timer. They can be rough.

MICHAEL. It's the chest-bumps I'm concerned with— *(Yells.)* It's okay, Frankie, pick yourself up, you're okay! *(DON is coaching first base.)*

DON *(yells)*. Top of the sixth, boys, last chance! *(To the runner.)* This is a big run, Philip! If Timmy hits it, you just keep running! Coach Mike is at third base, he'll tell you what to do! *(Beat.)* Go, Philip! Go! It's going all the way to the fence! Look at Coach Mike! *(MICHAEL is coaching third base.)*

MICHAEL. You can do it, Philip! I know you can do it!

DON. Don't watch the ball! Just run run run! *(MICHAEL waves Philip around to score.)*

MICHAEL. Hurry, Philip!

DON. Go, Philip!

MICHAEL. I mean, *go!* Don't slow down when you're rounding third! You can make it, all the way home! Go, Philip, go!

DON. Go! Go! Go!

MICHAEL. For God sakes, go! *(MICHAEL and DON watch, full of hope. The game is over. MICHAEL goes over to address the team.)* I am so proud of you guys. You played the game of your lives. I hope you never forget this season. I know I won't. Now go shake hands with the other team. We've got some great snacks, Linda's famous homemade health bars! *(MICHAEL and DON sit on the bench.)* I guess I shouldn't have sent Philip home.

DON. He would have made it easy it he didn't trip.

MICHAEL. All season long he was so resistant to double-knotting. I don't know why.

DON. Hey, did you see what happened after Philip was out? He went to the end of the bench and just sat there all alone. And then Timor went over and sat with him and then Eric went over and sat with him and then Frankie.

MICHAEL. I didn't even notice. What did they say?

DON. They didn't say anything. They didn't have to say anything. They were just there.

MICHAEL. They were all there, rooting for each other, the whole game. And nobody cried.

DON. They were a team.

MICHAEL. I love our team.

DON. I love our team too. And what about Frankie's catch?

MICHAEL. Oh, he had it all the way.

DON. Still, it was an important catch. If he hadn't made that catch we'd have lost by more than five runs.

MICHAEL. So, are you around town next week, Don?

DON. Yeah, if I can find a good parking place. Otherwise I'll have to put the van out at the gravel pit. Why?

MICHAEL. I'll call you.

DON. Why?

MICHAEL. We could maybe get together or something.

DON. Why?

MICHAEL. You know, hang out. Get a pizza. Whatever it is people do when they get together.

DON. I'm going to say something here, Mike.

MICHAEL. Okay.

DON. There's really no reason to get together.

MICHAEL. No?

DON. See, I don't really consider you a friend. And I think if you're honest with yourself, you'll find that you don't really consider me a friend, either.

MICHAEL. Yes I do! Of course I do! Why do you think I don't?

DON. Mike, please. I'm asking something from you. I'm asking you to be honest. That's a hard thing.

MICHAEL. So I shouldn't call you?

DON. I just don't know why you would. We had some good times out here coaching but the season's over.

MICHAEL. I really thought we were starting to become friends.

DON. I thought Tony was my friend. See, Mike, there comes a time for every man who lives in his van when he wants to know the truth. And the truth is, you and I could never be friends. And yes, I'll say "Hello, Mike," if I see you at the Food Emporium, but that's really no different than if I stopped to pat my neighbor's dog.

MICHAEL. To tell you the truth, there were many times I dreaded coming to the field because it meant seeing you.

I never knew what to say. Driving over, say I got stopped in traffic, I'd think about possible topics of conversation. It's kind of a relief to stop trying so hard.

DON. See? Isn't this better than some bullshit friendship where you have to fake stuff like caring about the other person? It's a pretty big thing we can tell each other the truth, Mike.

MICHAEL. I never thought not being friends would offer so much.

DON. Damn! I forgot to give out the snacks.

MICHAEL. I myself am pretty hungry. Unless you were going to take them to eat at a friend's house.

DON. No, help yourself. *(DON and MICHAEL sit on the bench and start eating the snacks.)*

MICHAEL. Great snacks, Don.

DON. I figured last game, our kids deserve good snacks. So I broke into the house in the middle of the night, cooked these up myself.

MICHAEL. That's a positive step. It means you and Linda were spending time together at home, even if she didn't know about it.

DON. It was nice to be back. After I cooked I walked around downstairs and sat in all my favorite chairs. Then, when I got out to the van, I threw a hammer at the house.

MICHAEL. How come?

DON. It was right there handy on the front seat.

MICHAEL. These things take time. *(Then.)* Are you sure all this equipment fits in the bag?

DON. It did last year. Let's see what we can do, Mike. *(DON and MICHAEL sit on the bench in silence, not ready to let the season end. FADE TO BLACK.)*

**END OF PLAY**